THE LAST PURR:
A Compassionate Guide to End-of-Life Cat Care

Nafisa Zareen Khan

First Paperback edition – December 2024
Published by Nafisa Khan Designs www.NafisaKhanDesigns.com

ISBN: 978-1966575023

For permissions, inquiries, or licensing requests, please contact the publisher at: nafisa@NafisaKhanDesigns.com

Thank you for supporting the author's rights and independent publishing.

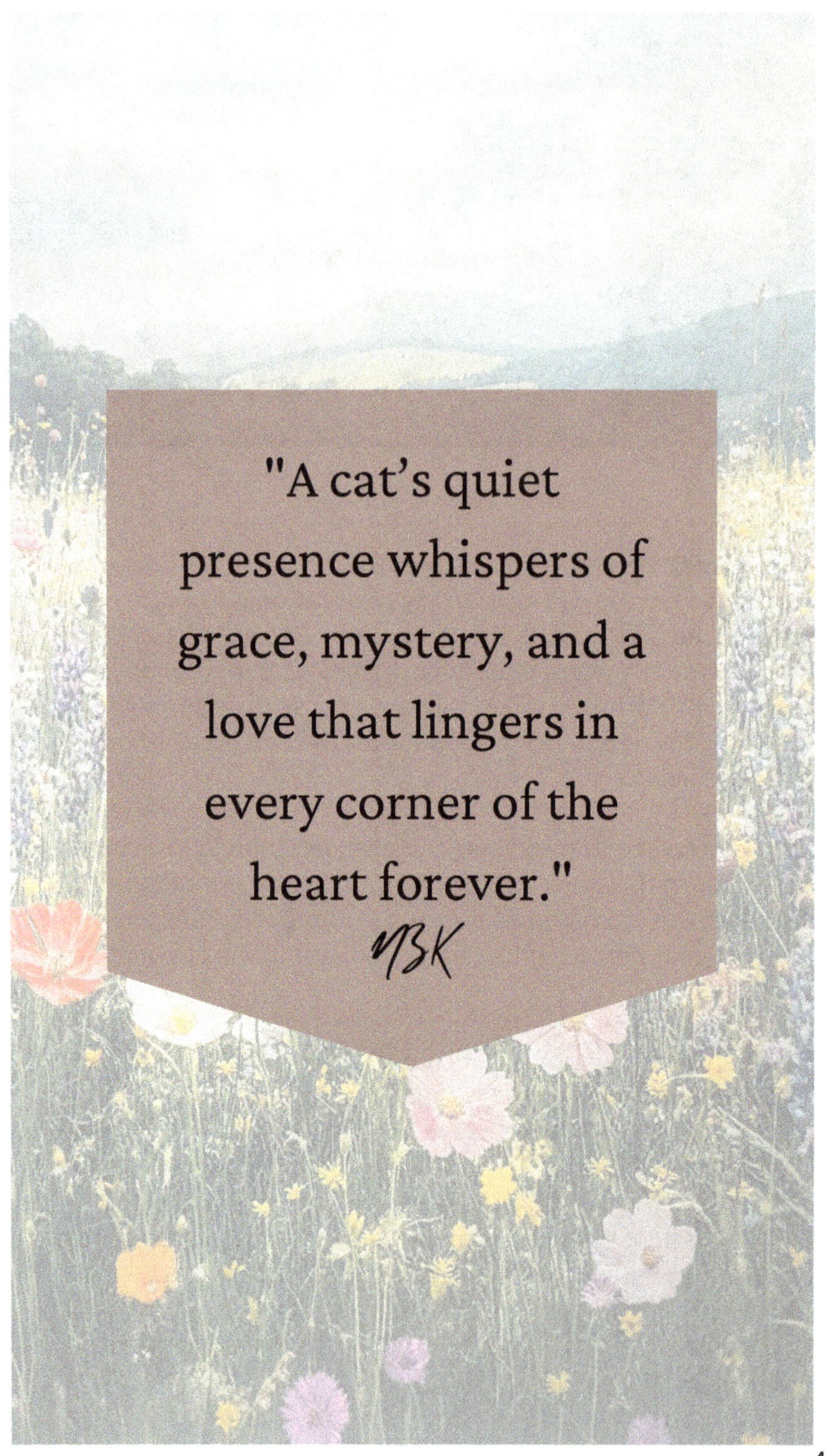
"A cat's quiet
presence whispers of
grace, mystery, and a
love that lingers in
every corner of the
heart forever."
NBK

Disclaimer

The information provided in this book is intended for educational and informational purposes only and should not be considered as professional veterinary advice. While every effort has been made to ensure the accuracy and reliability of the content, the author and publisher are not veterinarians or medical professionals. Readers should consult a qualified veterinarian for specific advice regarding their cat's health, behavior, or end-of-life care.

This book includes discussions of alternative therapies and treatments. Readers are strongly encouraged to consult with a licensed veterinarian before implementing any new treatment or therapy, especially those involving medications, supplements, or holistic practices.

The author and publisher assume no liability for any outcomes resulting from the application or misapplication of the information contained within this book. The care and well-being of your cat should always be guided by the expertise of a trusted veterinary professional.

By reading this book, you acknowledge and accept that the responsibility for your cat's care ultimately rests with you and your chosen veterinary care team.

Dedication

To every cat who has ever shared our homes, our hearts, and our lives.

Some stayed for many years. Others for far too short a time. Yet each left behind paw prints that can never be erased.

They greeted us at the door, curled beside us through life's joys and sorrows, and offered comfort without ever speaking a word. They taught us patience, trust, resilience, and the quiet beauty of simply being present. Through their gentle purrs, playful antics, and steadfast companionship, they became family.

Though their time with us was never long enough, their love endures in the memories we cherish, the habits we still smile about, and the empty places they once filled so completely.

This book is dedicated to the cats we have loved and lost, whose lives changed us forever and whose presence continues to echo in our hearts long after their final purr.

You were, and always will be, deeply loved.

Introduction

My bond with cats began in the spring of 1996 while I was stationed in Ansbach, Germany, during my service in the United States Army. There, I welcomed an eight week old tabby kitten named Bella into my life. What began as a simple companionship soon became one of the most meaningful relationships I would ever know. After returning to California, Bella remained faithfully by my side through life's triumphs, challenges, and countless ordinary moments that became extraordinary simply because she was there.

In 2014, I faced one of the most difficult decisions a pet owner can make: helping Bella find peace at the end of her life. The loss was profound, leaving a grief that lingered long after her final purr. Her passing changed me forever and deepened my understanding of the extraordinary bond we share with our animal companions.

Today, my home is filled with the love and companionship of five cherished cats, each with a unique personality and place in my heart. As my oldest cat enters her senior years and begins to show the natural signs of aging, I find myself preparing once again for a journey every devoted pet owner must eventually face. Motivated by both love and experience, I have spent countless hours researching ways to provide comfort, dignity, and compassionate care during a cat's final chapter.

This book is the result of that journey. My hope is to offer guidance, reassurance, and practical support to those caring for an aging or terminally ill feline companion. Sharing your life with a cat is a privilege built on unconditional love, trust, and companionship. In return, we owe them comfort, dignity, and compassion when they need us most. Whether you are exploring veterinary treatment options, considering holistic approaches, or facing difficult end of life decisions, I hope the information in these pages helps you navigate this deeply emotional time with confidence, grace, and love.

TABLE OF CONTENTS

Understanding the Aging Process 13

Providing Comfort and Care 29

Holistic and Alternative Therapies 53

Recognizing Signs of Decline 73

End-of-Life Care Options 83

Coping with the Loss of a Beloved Cat 93

Moving Forward 107

Trackers & Logs 113

Reflection Journal 135

Online Support Groups 149

Glossary 151

References 153

01 Understanding the Aging Process in Cats

- Physical Changes in Senior Cats...16
- Behavioral Changes in Senior Cats...22
- Why Understanding Aging Matters...27

Chapter One
Understanding the Aging Process in Cats

Sharing your life with a cat is a journey filled with joy, companionship, and deep emotional bonds. From the moment you welcome a cat into your home, they become more than just a pet—they become a cherished part of your family. Their unique personality, playful antics, and quiet companionship create a bond that deepens with time. Whether they're curling up in your lap, greeting you at the door, or simply being a calming presence in the room, the love of a cat is both profound and transformative.

As your feline friend ages, especially upon reaching their senior years, it's natural to seek ways to provide the best care, ensuring their comfort and dignity during their final days.
The aging process brings changes that can be both physical and emotional for your cat. While they may slow down, their need for love, attention, and understanding grows stronger. As a caregiver, you have the unique opportunity to repay the years of unconditional love they've given you by ensuring their later years are as fulfilling and pain-free as possible. This stage of their life is a time for patience, gentleness, and unwavering care. It is also a period when their bond with you may deepen further, as your role evolves into that of a devoted advocate for their well-being.

This guide offers compassionate advice on supporting your elderly cat through this stage, exploring both medical and holistic approaches, and discussing the considerations surrounding end-of-life decisions. With insights into senior cat health, this guide delves into understanding the signs of aging, managing chronic conditions, and making adjustments to their environment to suit their changing needs. Alongside traditional veterinary care, holistic therapies such as massage, acupuncture, and gentle herbal remedies are explored, providing a comprehensive view of options that can enhance their quality of life. At its heart, this book is about celebrating the incredible bond you share with your cat, honoring their unique spirit, and ensuring they feel loved and cherished in every moment.

Physical Changes in Senior Cats

The aging process affects cats much as it does humans, with visible and internal changes becoming more apparent over time. These changes can influence their mobility, energy levels, and overall health, necessitating adjustments in care to support their well-being.

Decreased Mobility

As cats age, their joints and muscles often begin to show signs of wear and tear, leading to reduced mobility. Arthritis is particularly common in senior cats and can cause discomfort or difficulty performing daily activities. Even routine behaviors, such as jumping onto furniture or grooming, may become challenging.

Additional Symptoms to Monitor:

- Limping or favoring one leg.
- Reduced grooming, leading to matted or dull fur.
- Reluctance to climb stairs or jump down from heights.

How to Help:

- Provide ramps or steps to help them access favorite spots like beds or sofas.
- Offer a warm, cushioned resting area to alleviate pressure on their joints.
- Consult your veterinarian about joint supplements, such as glucosamine and chondroitin, or pain relief options tailored to their needs.

Notes:

Weight Fluctuations

Weight management becomes more challenging in senior cats. Muscle atrophy can result in weight loss, while conditions like decreased metabolism or reduced activity can cause weight gain. Both extremes can impact their health significantly.

Additional Symptoms to Monitor:

- Noticeable thinning along the spine and hindquarters.
- Difficulty walking or standing due to excess weight.
- Changes in appetite, such as overeating or refusing food.

How to Help:

- Adjust their diet to meet senior nutritional needs, focusing on high-protein, low-calorie foods for weight control.
- Incorporate gentle play to keep them active and maintain muscle tone.
- Schedule regular weigh-ins and checkups with your veterinarian to monitor progress.

Notes:

Sensory Decline

Aging affects a cat's vision, hearing, and sense of smell. These changes can alter their behavior, making them more hesitant in unfamiliar surroundings or causing them to appear disoriented.

Additional Symptoms to Monitor:

- Increased startle responses to unexpected touch due to reduced hearing.
- Misjudging distances when jumping or climbing.
- Disinterest in familiar toys or food due to diminished senses.

How to Help:

- Keep their environment consistent to reduce stress caused by sensory changes.
- Use nightlights to help them navigate in dim lighting.
- Call them gently or use vibrations (like tapping on the floor) to get their attention.

Notes:

"Understanding the aging process in cats is a journey of compassion, embracing their wisdom while adapting to their changing needs with love."

Dental Problems

Dental health often deteriorates in older cats, leading to chronic pain, difficulty eating, and an increased risk of systemic infections if left untreated. Regular dental care is essential to their overall well-being.

Additional Symptoms to Monitor:

- Excessive drooling or foul-smelling breath.
- Visible redness, swelling, or bleeding in the gums.
- Changes in eating habits, such as chewing on one side of the mouth or dropping food.

How to Help:

- Offer softer foods or warm their meals to make them easier to chew.
- Schedule annual dental cleanings with your veterinarian to address tartar buildup and gum disease.
- Use feline-specific dental gels or toys designed to improve oral hygiene.

Notes:

Changes in Coat and Skin

Senior cats often experience changes in the texture and appearance of their coat and skin. Their fur may become thinner or less shiny, and skin may lose elasticity.

Additional Symptoms to Monitor:

- Dry, flaky skin or bald patches.
- Increased sensitivity to touch in certain areas.
- Overgrooming or neglecting grooming altogether.

How to Help:

- Regularly groom your cat with a soft brush to maintain a healthy coat and improve circulation.
- Use hypoallergenic shampoos for sensitive skin, if bathing is necessary.
- Ensure they are well-hydrated, as dehydration can exacerbate skin issues.

By understanding these physical changes and responding proactively, you can help your senior cat maintain a higher quality of life. Always consult your veterinarian for tailored advice and treatment options to address specific concerns.

Notes:

Behavioral Changes in Senior Cats

As cats age, their behaviors often change in ways that reflect both their physical health and cognitive state. These shifts can include alterations in their social interactions, activity levels, and daily routines. Recognizing and adapting to these changes can help ensure your senior cat feels safe, comfortable, and loved during their later years.

Altered Sleep Patterns

Elderly cats tend to sleep more, sometimes up to 18–20 hours a day, as their energy levels decline. However, disruptions in their sleep patterns can also occur, such as restlessness or increased activity during the night. These changes may reflect underlying discomfort, cognitive decline, or other age-related issues.

Additional Symptoms to Monitor:

- Difficulty settling down before sleep or frequent changes in sleeping spots.
- Sleeping in unusual positions that suggest joint pain or discomfort.
- Increased vocalizations during the night, potentially signaling confusion or discomfort.

How to Help:

- Create a quiet, comfortable sleeping area with soft bedding and warm blankets.
- Maintain a consistent daily routine to support a natural sleep-wake cycle.
- Consult your veterinarian if sleep disruptions persist, as they could indicate pain or anxiety.

Notes:

Changes in Social Interaction

Social behavior often changes as cats age. Some may become more affectionate and seek constant reassurance, while others may withdraw and prefer solitude. These behaviors can be influenced by health issues, changes in sensory perception, or emotional needs.

Additional Symptoms to Monitor:

- Sudden changes in how your cat interacts with you or other pets.
- Increased hiding, especially in unfamiliar or quiet places.
- Seeking physical closeness, such as sitting on your lap more frequently or following you from room to room.

How to Help:

- Provide attention and affection on your cat's terms; avoid forcing interactions.
- Ensure they have access to quiet, safe spaces where they can retreat if needed.
- Use gentle words and petting to comfort them, especially if they seem clingy or anxious.

Notes:

Cognitive Decline

Feline cognitive dysfunction (FCD), akin to dementia in humans, can affect a senior cat's memory, learning, and problem-solving abilities. Behavioral changes such as confusion, restlessness, or changes in routine are common.

Additional Symptoms to Monitor:

- Difficulty navigating familiar environments, such as getting stuck behind furniture or not recognizing family members.
- Reduced responsiveness to stimuli, like your voice or the sound of their name.
- Increased irritability or anxiety, often manifesting as vocalizations or pacing.

How to Help:

- Keep their environment consistent by minimizing changes to furniture or routine.
- Use nightlights to help them navigate at night, reducing anxiety caused by darkness.
- Provide interactive toys or food puzzles to stimulate their mind and combat boredom.

Notes:

Litter Box Issues

Senior cats may face challenges with litter box use due to mobility limitations, cognitive decline, or medical conditions such as arthritis or urinary tract infections. These issues can lead to accidents, avoidance, or visible distress when using the box.

Additional Symptoms to Monitor:

- Straining or discomfort when using the litter box.
- Frequent urination outside the box, possibly indicating urinary issues.
- Sitting near the litter box without attempting to use it.

How to Help:

- Switch to low-sided litter boxes that are easier for them to access.
- Place multiple litter boxes in easily accessible locations throughout your home.
- Use soft, fine-grain litter to reduce discomfort on sensitive paws.

Notes:

Changes in Grooming Habits

Senior cats may neglect their grooming routines due to stiffness, reduced mobility, or lack of energy. This can lead to matting, dandruff, or an unkempt coat. Conversely, some may overgroom out of stress or discomfort.

Additional Symptoms to Monitor:

- Increased matting or clumps of fur, especially in hard-to-reach areas like the back or hindquarters.
- Redness or irritation from overgrooming.
- Decreased attention to their claws, leading to overgrown nails.

How to Help:

- Brush your cat regularly with a gentle brush designed for sensitive skin.
- Use grooming wipes to clean areas they can no longer reach.
- Schedule regular nail trims to prevent overgrowth and discomfort.

Understanding and responding to these behavioral changes is key to ensuring your senior cat's happiness and well-being. By observing their needs closely and making small adjustments, you can help them navigate the challenges of aging with dignity and comfort. Always consult your veterinarian for tailored advice and support.

Why Understanding Aging Matters

Recognizing the signs of aging in your cat is not just about addressing physical changes—it's about preserving their quality of life and strengthening the bond you share during their golden years. Cats age gracefully, but their needs evolve, and being attentive to these changes can make a significant difference in their comfort and happiness.

By observing your cat closely, you can identify subtle changes in their behavior, mobility, or overall health that may signal the need for intervention. For example, a once-active cat that now hesitates to jump onto furniture may be experiencing joint pain, while a sudden increase in vocalizations could indicate discomfort or cognitive decline. Early recognition of these signs allows you to consult with your veterinarian and develop a care plan tailored to your cat's specific needs.

Addressing health issues promptly can prevent minor concerns from escalating into major problems. Whether it's adjusting their diet, creating a more accessible environment, or incorporating therapies to manage pain, proactive care ensures your cat remains comfortable and content. This also includes emotional well-being, as senior cats often require more attention and reassurance to feel secure in their changing bodies.

Understanding aging is not just about making physical adjustments but also about celebrating the time you have together. It's an opportunity to deepen the trust and love you've built over the years by providing them with the care and compassion they deserve. By adapting to their needs with patience and love, you can ensure that their twilight years are as fulfilling and joyful as the rest of their life.

Notes:

"Cats are the quiet poets of our hearts, speaking volumes through their gentle purrs and knowing eyes."

02 Providing Comfort and Care

- Pain Management...32
- Tailoring Nutrition for Senior Cats...36
- Environmental Modifications for a Senior-Friendly Home...40
- Enhancing Mental and Emotional Well-Being...45
- Veterinary Care...49

Chapter Two
Providing Comfort and Care

As your cat enters their senior years, comfort becomes a priority. Aging brings about physical, emotional, and behavioral changes that can affect your cat's quality of life. It is during this stage that your role as a caregiver becomes even more critical, as you help them navigate these changes with love, patience, and understanding.

Providing them with an environment tailored to their changing needs is one of the most impactful ways to ensure their well-being. Senior cats benefit from a calm, predictable environment where their physical limitations are accommodated. This includes creating easy access to their favorite resting spots, food, water, and litter boxes, as well as ensuring safety through adjustments like ramps, soft bedding, and secure surroundings.

Addressing potential health challenges is equally vital. Senior cats are prone to conditions such as arthritis, kidney disease, or dental issues, which can cause discomfort or pain if left untreated. Regular veterinary checkups, combined with close observation of their behavior and appetite, can help you catch these issues early and provide effective treatment. Pain management, proper nutrition, and mental stimulation play key roles in helping your cat feel secure and happy.

Emotional well-being is just as important as physical care. Senior cats often seek more reassurance and affection as they age. Spending quality time with them, offering enrichment activities, and maintaining a consistent daily routine can help reduce anxiety and provide a sense of stability.

This chapter delves into various strategies to ensure your elderly cat feels secure, loved, and pain-free. By addressing their unique needs with compassion and proactive care, you can help your feline companion enjoy their golden years with dignity and joy.

Pain Management

Pain management is a cornerstone of care for senior cats, as it directly impacts their quality of life. Cats are experts at hiding discomfort, so it's vital to recognize subtle signs of pain and address them promptly. Whether they're dealing with arthritis, dental issues, or other chronic conditions, alleviating pain ensures they can enjoy their remaining years with comfort and dignity.

Medications

Veterinarians may prescribe medications tailored specifically for feline pain management. These may include non-steroidal anti-inflammatory drugs (NSAIDs) or other pain relievers that target inflammation and discomfort. Always follow veterinary advice, as improper use of medications can be harmful.

Key Points to Remember:

- ***NSAIDs for Cats Only:*** Medications like meloxicam are commonly prescribed for feline arthritis but must be dosed carefully to avoid side effects.
- ***Gabapentin:*** Often used for managing chronic pain or anxiety associated with veterinary visits.
- ***Opioids:*** In severe cases, short-term opioid medications may be prescribed for acute pain relief.
- ***Never Use Human Medications:*** Medications such as acetaminophen (Tylenol) or ibuprofen are toxic to cats and can be fatal.

How You Can Help:

- Monitor your cat for signs of side effects, such as vomiting or lethargy, and report them to your veterinarian.
- Follow the prescribed dosage and schedule rigorously.
- Combine medication with other therapies for comprehensive pain relief.

Notes:

Alternative Therapies

For a holistic approach to pain management, alternative therapies can complement traditional medications. These non-invasive treatments are increasingly recognized for their effectiveness in improving mobility, reducing inflammation, and enhancing overall well-being.

Acupuncture

Acupuncture involves inserting thin needles into specific points on the body to stimulate nerve endings and promote healing. This therapy can alleviate pain caused by arthritis or other chronic conditions.

Benefits:

- Increases circulation and reduces inflammation.
- Stimulates the release of natural pain-relieving endorphins.

What to Consider:

- Only allow a certified veterinary acupuncturist to perform the procedure.
- Sessions may need to be repeated for lasting benefits.

Laser Therapy

Low-level laser therapy, also known as cold laser therapy, uses light to penetrate tissues and reduce inflammation.

Benefits:

- Promotes tissue repair and regeneration.
- Can be used for a variety of conditions, including joint pain and wound healing.

What to Consider:

- Requires multiple sessions for noticeable results.
- Often used in conjunction with other treatments.

Notes:

Alternative Therapies

CBD Oil

Cannabidiol (CBD) has gained popularity in recent years as a natural remedy for pets dealing with chronic pain, anxiety, and inflammation.

Potential Benefits:

- ***Pain and Inflammation Relief:*** CBD interacts with the body's endocannabinoid system to reduce pain and inflammation associated with conditions like arthritis and injury.
- ***Improved Sleep:*** Older cats often struggle with restlessness. CBD can promote deeper, more restorative sleep.
- ***Anxiety Reduction:*** For cats with anxiety or stress-related behaviors, CBD offers a calming effect.

Dosage and Safety:

- Start with a low dose and gradually adjust based on your cat's response.
- Use only CBD products specifically designed for pets, as human-grade CBD may contain unsafe ingredients like THC.
- Monitor for adverse effects such as vomiting, lethargy, or changes in appetite, and discontinue use if any occur.

Notes:

Alternative Therapies

Massage

Gentle massage can ease muscle tension, improve circulation, and provide relaxation for senior cats.

Benefits:

- Enhances flexibility and mobility.
- Strengthens the bond between you and your cat.

How to Perform Safely:

- Use light, circular motions, avoiding areas that seem sensitive or painful.
- Seek guidance from a professional animal massage therapist for proper techniques.

Notes:

Tailoring Nutrition for Senior Cats

Proper nutrition is vital for maintaining your cat's health and energy levels, especially as they age. Senior cats often have unique dietary requirements due to changes in metabolism, activity levels, and the development of age-related health issues. Tailoring their diet can significantly enhance their quality of life and support their overall well-being.

Balanced Diet

A well-balanced diet is the cornerstone of senior cat care. Aging cats often benefit from specially formulated senior cat food that addresses their specific nutritional needs.

Look for diets that:

- Include easily digestible proteins to support muscle maintenance and prevent weight loss. Protein is crucial for older cats, but it must be of high quality to reduce strain on their kidneys.
- Contain omega-3 fatty acids to promote joint health, reduce inflammation, and support a shiny coat.
- Are fortified with essential vitamins and minerals, such as vitamin E for immune support and taurine for heart health.
- Have moderate calorie content to prevent weight gain from reduced activity levels.

How to Choose the Right Food:

- Opt for brands that specialize in senior formulas with clear labeling.
- Consult your veterinarian about prescription diets if your cat has conditions like kidney disease, diabetes, or hyperthyroidism.
- Introduce new food gradually over 7–10 days to prevent digestive upset.

Notes:

Hydration

Hydration becomes increasingly important as cats age, especially for those prone to kidney disease or urinary tract issues. Senior cats are more susceptible to dehydration, which can exacerbate existing health problems.

How to Encourage Hydration:

- ***Provide fresh water daily:*** Use wide, shallow bowls that don't touch your cat's whiskers to encourage drinking.
- ***Incorporate wet food:*** Wet food has a high moisture content, making it an excellent way to boost hydration.
- ***Use water fountains:*** Many cats are attracted to running water, which can increase their intake.
- ***Add water to dry food:*** Mixing warm water or low-sodium chicken broth into dry kibble can enhance flavor and improve hydration.

Notes:

Supplements

Supplements can play a vital role in supporting your senior cat's health, especially when combined with a balanced diet. However, always consult your veterinarian before introducing any supplements to ensure they are appropriate for your cat's specific needs.

Common Supplements for Senior Cats:

- ***Glucosamine and Chondroitin:*** Help maintain joint health, reduce stiffness, and alleviate arthritis symptoms.
- ***Omega-3 Fatty Acids:*** Reduce inflammation and support heart, skin, and joint health.
- ***Probiotics:*** Improve digestion and support a healthy gut microbiome, especially for cats prone to gastrointestinal issues.
- ***Taurine:*** Essential for maintaining healthy vision, heart function, and overall well-being.
- ***Vitamin B Complex:*** Can help boost energy levels and support nerve function in aging cats.

Notes:

Tailoring the Diet for Specific Health Conditions

Senior cats often develop health conditions that require special dietary considerations:

- ***Kidney Disease:*** Opt for low-protein, low-phosphorus diets to reduce the strain on the kidneys.
- ***Diabetes:*** High-protein, low-carbohydrate diets can help regulate blood sugar levels.
- ***Obesity:*** Look for weight management formulas that provide balanced nutrition with fewer calories.
- ***Dental Issues:*** Softer foods, such as wet or moistened kibble, can make eating easier for cats with dental pain.

Monitoring Your Cat's Nutritional Health

Regularly monitor your cat's weight, appetite, and overall condition to ensure their diet meets their needs. If you notice changes such as weight loss, lethargy, or vomiting, consult your veterinarian immediately to adjust their diet accordingly.

Proper nutrition is not only about meeting their physical needs but also about enhancing their comfort and happiness. By providing the right diet and hydration, you can help your senior cat thrive in their golden years.

Notes:

Environmental Modifications for a Senior-Friendly Home

Creating a senior-friendly home can make a significant difference in your cat's comfort, safety, and overall well-being. Small adjustments tailored to their needs can help reduce stress, prevent injuries, and enhance their quality of life as they age.

Accessible Resources

Making essential resources easily accessible minimizes strain on your senior cat and ensures they can go about their daily activities comfortably.

How to Adjust:

- ***Place Food, Water, and Litter Boxes Strategically:*** Ensure these items are available on each level of your home, so your cat doesn't need to navigate stairs or long distances.
- ***Low-Sided Litter Boxes:*** Choose litter boxes with low sides to accommodate cats with mobility issues or arthritis. Consider cutting a small opening in one side for even easier access.
- ***Elevated Food and Water Bowls:*** Use slightly raised bowls to reduce neck strain, especially for cats with joint pain.

Additional Tips:

- Ensure their litter box is in a quiet, low-traffic area to reduce stress.
- Keep food and water stations clean and replenished daily to encourage hydration and proper nutrition.

Notes:

Comfortable Resting Areas

Rest is essential for senior cats, and creating cozy, supportive resting spots can make a significant impact on their comfort.

How to Adjust:

- ***Provide Orthopedic or Heated Beds:*** Orthopedic mats or memory foam beds offer joint support and relieve pressure points, while heated beds can soothe arthritis pain.
- ***Choose Quiet Locations:*** Set up resting areas in warm, quiet corners away from drafts, loud noises, or high foot traffic.
- ***Create Multiple Options:*** Offer several resting spots throughout your home so your cat can choose a location that suits their mood and needs.

Additional Tips:

- Add soft blankets or cushions to their favorite sleeping spots.
- Wash bedding regularly to keep it fresh and free from allergens or odors.

Notes:

Safety Enhancements

Senior cats often experience reduced vision, hearing, and mobility, which can make navigating their environment more challenging. Safety modifications can prevent accidents and create a more secure space for them.

How to Adjust:

- ***Remove Tripping Hazards:*** Keep walkways clear of clutter, loose cords, or small objects that could cause your cat to trip or stumble.
- ***Secure Furniture:*** Anchor wobbly furniture or unstable shelves to prevent them from tipping over if your cat leans or jumps on them.
- ***Install Ramps or Steps:*** Ramps or pet stairs can help your cat access elevated areas, such as sofas, beds, or window perches, without straining their joints.
- ***Ensure Proper Lighting:*** Use nightlights or keep dim lights on to help cats with declining vision navigate safely, especially in hallways or near litter boxes.

Additional Tips:

- Avoid moving furniture around unnecessarily, as senior cats rely on familiarity to feel secure.
- Use non-slip mats or rugs in areas with slippery floors to give your cat better traction.

Notes:

Enhancing Emotional Security

In addition to physical modifications, creating a calm and reassuring environment can help senior cats feel more at ease.

How to Adjust:

- ***Use Calming Scents or Pheromones:*** Products like feline pheromone diffusers can create a sense of security and reduce anxiety.
- ***Keep Familiar Items Nearby:*** Blankets, toys, or scratching posts they've used for years provide comfort and familiarity.
- ***Offer Gentle Stimulation:*** Place their bed near a window with a view of birds or trees to provide mental stimulation without requiring physical effort.

By adapting your home to meet the needs of your senior cat, you can ensure they remain safe, comfortable, and happy in their golden years. These thoughtful modifications demonstrate your love and care while allowing your feline companion to age with dignity and ease.

Notes:

"Providing comfort and care to a cat in the final stages of their live is the purest act of love, offering peace and presence in their final moments."

Enhancing Mental and Emotional Well-Being

Caring for your senior cat's mental health is just as important as addressing their physical needs. As cats age, their cognitive abilities and emotional resilience may change, making it crucial to provide a supportive and engaging environment that nurtures their mental and emotional well-being.

Quality Time Together

Spending meaningful time with your senior cat is one of the most effective ways to support their emotional well-being.

How to Strengthen Your Bond:

- ***Affectionate Interaction:*** Provide plenty of pets, cuddles, and gentle brushing sessions. Many senior cats crave more attention as they age, seeking reassurance and comfort.
- ***Calm and Reassuring Presence:*** Sit quietly with your cat while reading, working, or relaxing. Your presence can provide them with a sense of security and companionship.
- ***Respect Their Preferences:*** Allow your cat to dictate the level of interaction. Some cats may prefer quiet companionship overactive play, and honoring their wishes helps them feel safe and understood.

Notes:

Enrichment Activities

Enrichment activities help keep your senior cat mentally stimulated, engaged, and happy. Even if they are less active than they were in their younger years, mental stimulation can prevent boredom, reduce anxiety, and promote a sense of purpose.

Ideas for Enrichment:

- ***Interactive Toys and Puzzles:*** Offer puzzle feeders or treat-dispensing toys to encourage problem-solving and reward-seeking behavior. These activities stimulate their mind while satisfying their natural hunting instincts.
- ***Gentle Play Sessions:*** Use slow-moving toys like feather wands or ribbons to engage your cat in gentle, low-impact play. Adjust the intensity to their energy level to avoid overstressing their joints or muscles.
- ***Cat TV or Nature Sounds:*** Set up a spot near a window where your cat can watch birds, squirrels, or other outdoor activity. Alternatively, play nature videos or calming sounds to entertain and soothe them.
- ***Scratching Posts and Cat Trees:*** Even senior cats benefit from scratching as it helps maintain claw health and provides a satisfying physical activity. Ensure posts are stable and easy to access.

Benefits:

- Encourages mental stimulation and prevents cognitive decline.
- Reduces anxiety and stress by keeping them occupied.
- Strengthens the bond between you and your cat through interactive play.

Notes:

Consistency

Older cats thrive on routine. Maintaining predictable schedules and familiar environments reduces stress and fosters a sense of stability.

How to Create a Routine:

- ***Regular Feeding Times:*** Serve meals at the same time each day. Senior cats often become creatures of habit, and consistent mealtimes help reduce anxiety.
- ***Set Play Sessions:*** Schedule short playtimes at predictable intervals to give them something to look forward to.
- ***Stable Sleeping Arrangements:*** Avoid moving their bedding or favorite resting spots unnecessarily. Familiarity is comforting to senior cats, particularly those experiencing cognitive decline.

Benefits of Consistency:

- Builds trust and reduces anxiety in cats who may be more easily startled or disoriented.
- Helps them adapt to physical or cognitive changes with less stress.
- Creates a calm, predictable environment that promotes relaxation and well-being.

Notes:

Additional Tips for Emotional Support

- ***Pheromone Diffusers:*** Products like Feliway can help create a calming atmosphere by mimicking natural feline pheromones.
- ***Limit Changes:*** Avoid introducing new pets, rearranging furniture, or creating disruptions in their environment. Gradual transitions are key when changes are necessary.
- ***Monitor for Signs of Stress:*** Watch for behaviors like hiding, excessive grooming, or loss of appetite, which may indicate anxiety or depression.

Supporting your senior cat's mental and emotional well-being ensures they remain happy, engaged, and connected with you as they age. Through consistent care, meaningful interaction, and engaging activities, you can provide the love and reassurance they need to thrive in their golden years.

Notes:

Veterinary Care

Regular veterinary visits become increasingly critical as your cat ages. Senior cats are more susceptible to various health conditions, and early detection through routine checkups can make a significant difference in their quality of life. A proactive approach to veterinary care ensures that health issues are addressed promptly, helping your cat remain comfortable, happy, and active during their golden years.

Preventive Care

Preventive care is essential for maintaining your senior cat's overall health and preventing the progression of age-related conditions.

Steps for Preventive Care:

- ***Vaccinations:*** Keep vaccinations up to date based on your veterinarian's recommendations. While older cats may not need all the vaccines younger cats require, some, like the rabies vaccine, are crucial for their safety. Discuss tailored vaccination schedules with your vet.

- ***Routine Monitoring:*** Pay close attention to changes in weight, appetite, and behavior, as these may indicate underlying health problems. For example, sudden weight loss could signal hyperthyroidism, while decreased appetite might point to dental pain or gastrointestinal issues.

- ***Parasite Prevention:*** Continue to protect your cat from fleas, ticks, and internal parasites, as their immune system may be less robust in their senior years. Opt for vet-recommended parasite preventatives that are safe for older cats.

- ***Dental Care:*** Poor dental health can lead to pain and systemic infections. Regularly inspect your cat's mouth for signs of tartar, bad breath, or gum inflammation and discuss professional cleanings with your vet.

Notes:

Diagnostic Tests

Senior cats often develop conditions like kidney disease, diabetes, arthritis, or hyperthyroidism as they age. Diagnostic tests are crucial for identifying these issues early, even before symptoms become apparent.

Common Diagnostic Tests:

- ***Bloodwork:*** Routine blood tests, including a complete blood count (CBC) and biochemistry panel, help monitor organ function and detect conditions like kidney disease or diabetes. Elevated creatinine or blood glucose levels are early indicators of these issues.
- ***Urine Analysis:*** A urinalysis can detect infections, crystals, or kidney issues. It provides valuable information about your cat's hydration status and overall urinary tract health.
- ***Thyroid Function Tests:*** Senior cats are prone to hyperthyroidism, a condition that can cause weight loss, increased appetite, and hyperactivity. Thyroid hormone (T4) tests can diagnose this condition early.
- ***Blood Pressure Monitoring:*** High blood pressure is common in older cats and can lead to serious complications like blindness or kidney damage. Regular monitoring can help manage this condition.
- ***Imaging:*** X-rays or ultrasounds may be recommended to evaluate joint health, detect tumors, or examine internal organs for abnormalities.

Benefits of Regular Diagnostic Tests:

- Early detection of illnesses allows for timely interventions, which can slow disease progression.
- Helps your veterinarian create a personalized treatment or management plan tailored to your cat's specific needs.

Notes:

Additional Veterinary Care Tips

- ***Semi-Annual Checkups:*** While annual visits may suffice for younger cats, senior cats benefit from checkups every six months. These frequent visits ensure that even subtle changes in their health are caught early.
- ***Pain Management:*** If your cat has arthritis or other chronic conditions, discuss pain management options, including medications, supplements, or alternative therapies like acupuncture.
- ***Grooming Assistance:*** Cats with arthritis or mobility issues may struggle to groom themselves. Your veterinarian can advise on appropriate grooming techniques or recommend skin and coat care products.
- ***End-of-Life Planning:*** Open communication with your veterinarian about your cat's quality of life is vital. They can guide you on hospice care, palliative treatments, or making compassionate end-of-life decisions when the time comes.

By implementing these care strategies and maintaining a close partnership with your veterinarian, you can ensure that your senior cat remains healthy, comfortable, and well-loved throughout their later years. Regular veterinary care not only addresses existing health concerns but also provides peace of mind, knowing you are giving your feline companion the best possible support during this stage of life.

Notes:

"Having a pet cat is a gift of quiet companionship, where every purr and playful glance fills your life with warmth and joy."

03

Holistic and Alternative Therapies

- Acupuncture...56
- Massage Therapy...57
- CBD Oil Therapy...60
- Herbal Remedies...64
- Aromatherapy...67
- Hydrotherapy...69
- Energy Therapies...70
- Combining therapies for maximum comfort...71
- Monitoring Progress...71

Chapter Three
Holistic and Alternative Therapies

Caring for an elderly cat requires a deep understanding of their changing needs as they age. Beyond addressing their basic requirements such as food, shelter, and hygiene, it's essential to recognize the emotional and physical challenges they may face. Aging cats often experience pain, anxiety, and reduced mobility, which can significantly affect their quality of life. By adopting a comprehensive care approach, pet owners can ensure their feline companions remain comfortable and happy in their later years, creating a nurturing environment where they feel secure and loved.

Integrating holistic and alternative therapies alongside traditional veterinary care can greatly enhance the care experience for both you and your cat. These therapies, such as acupuncture, massage, CBD oil, and aromatherapy, provide targeted solutions for common issues like chronic pain, inflammation, and stress. They not only help address specific health concerns but also improve overall well-being by focusing on relaxation, circulation, and emotional balance. By incorporating these practices, you can foster a deeper connection with your cat while ensuring their physical needs are met in a gentle, non-invasive manner.

The beauty of holistic therapies lies in their ability to complement conventional treatments, offering a multi-dimensional approach to feline care. Whether it's calming anxiety with aromatherapy, alleviating joint pain through acupuncture, or simply creating a peaceful atmosphere with Reiki or gentle massage, these methods prioritize your cat's comfort and emotional health. Such practices not only help alleviate discomfort but also promote a serene bond between you and your pet, making the final stages of their life as meaningful and joyful as possible.

Acupuncture

Acupuncture is an ancient practice that has found modern application in veterinary medicine, offering relief for various chronic conditions.

Benefits:

- ***Pain Management:*** Acupuncture is highly effective in addressing chronic pain, including conditions like arthritis, neurological disorders, and injuries.
- ***Improved Healing:*** By increasing blood flow and stimulating the nervous system, acupuncture can enhance the body's natural healing process.
- ***Behavioral Benefits:*** Cats undergoing acupuncture often appear calmer and more relaxed, as the release of endorphins can reduce anxiety.

How It Works:

- Fine needles are gently inserted into specific acupuncture points, which correspond to areas of energy flow (meridians) in the body.
- The process requires skill and expertise. A certified veterinary acupuncturist ensures the procedure is not only effective but also minimally stressful for the cat.

Advanced Applications:

- ***Electroacupuncture:*** A gentle electrical current is passed through the needles for enhanced stimulation, particularly useful for severe pain or nerve damage.
- ***Laser Acupuncture:*** For needle-averse cats, lasers can be used to stimulate the same points without puncturing the skin.

Notes:

Massage Therapy

Massage therapy is a soothing, hands-on approach to improving your cat's physical comfort, emotional well-being, and overall health. Regular massage can help address specific health concerns while strengthening the bond between you and your cat.

Benefits:

- ***Improved Circulation:*** Gentle massage promotes blood flow, which enhances healing, reduces swelling, and helps deliver oxygen and nutrients to tissues. This is particularly beneficial for cats recovering from injury or surgery.
- ***Stress Reduction:*** The calming touch of massage helps relieve anxiety and promotes a sense of security, making it especially useful for nervous or senior cats.
- ***Pain Relief:*** Massage can help reduce muscle tension and alleviate discomfort in cats suffering from arthritis, hip dysplasia, or other chronic conditions.
- ***Enhanced Flexibility:*** Regular massage sessions can maintain joint flexibility and prevent stiffness, which is especially beneficial for older or less active cats.

Techniques:

- ***Effleurage:*** Use light, smooth strokes along the cat's back, sides, and legs to relax muscles, improve blood flow, and create a sense of calm.
- ***Kneading:*** With gentle pressure, mimic the motion cats make with their paws to ease tension in specific areas, such as the shoulders or hips.
- ***Passive Stretching:*** Carefully guide your cat's limbs to stretch muscles and joints, improving flexibility and range of motion, particularly in arthritic or aging cats.
- ***Circular Movements:*** Use small, circular motions with your fingertips to gently massage areas like the shoulders, base of the tail, and neck, which are common tension spots.

Notes:

Massage Therapy

Techniques...

- ***Head and Chin Massage:*** Rub the area around your cat's cheeks, forehead, and chin using slow, rhythmic strokes. This is especially soothing for cats that enjoy face rubs.
- ***Tail Massage:*** Gently massage the base and length of the tail to relieve tension and promote relaxation but be cautious as some cats may be sensitive in this area.

Considerations:

- Pay close attention to your cat's body language and vocalizations to ensure they are comfortable and enjoying the process. Signs of discomfort include squirming, growling, or moving away.
- Avoid applying pressure to sensitive areas such as the stomach or spine, as these may cause discomfort or injury.
- Cats with severe health conditions, injuries, or recent surgeries should only be massaged by trained professionals or under veterinary guidance.
- Ensure the environment is calm and quiet, as sudden noises or distractions can stress your cat and hinder the benefits of the massage.
- Gradually introduce massage into your cat's routine, starting with short sessions and increasing the duration as they become accustomed to the process.
- Always consult with your veterinarian before beginning massage therapy, especially if your cat has medical conditions or is on treatment.

Notes:

"Holistic and alternative therapies for cats respect their innate wisdom, offering gentle care to support their well-being and balance."

CBD Oil

Cannabidiol (CBD) oil has gained significant attention as a potential option for managing pain, anxiety, and other health concerns in pets, including cats. Derived from the hemp plant, CBD oil is non-psychoactive and works by interacting with the endocannabinoid system, which regulates various physiological processes. While scientific research into its effects on cats is still evolving, many pet owners report noticeable improvements in their cat's comfort, mobility, and overall demeanor when using CBD products.

Forms of CBD for Cats

CBD products are available in various forms, allowing you to choose the one that best suits your cat's preferences and needs.

Options Include:

- ***CBD Oil Tinctures:*** Easy to administer, tinctures can be added to your cat's food, water, or given directly using a dropper.
- ***CBD Treats:*** Pre-measured treats are a convenient way to incorporate CBD into your cat's diet, but ensure they contain high-quality ingredients.
- ***Topical CBD Creams:*** These can be applied to specific areas, such as joints, for localized relief from pain or inflammation.

Notes:

CBD Oil

Benefits of CBD Oil

CBD oil offers several potential benefits for senior cats, particularly those dealing with chronic conditions or age-related challenges.

Key Benefits:

- ***Reduces Inflammation:*** CBD oil has anti-inflammatory properties, making it helpful for managing arthritis and other conditions that cause joint pain or stiffness.
- ***Supports Pain Management:*** By interacting with receptors that modulate pain, CBD oil may alleviate discomfort associated with chronic illnesses, injuries, or aging.
- ***Promotes Relaxation:*** Senior cats often experience anxiety or restlessness due to cognitive decline or environmental changes. CBD oil can help calm their nerves and improve their overall sense of well-being.
- ***Encourages Appetite:*** Cats dealing with nausea, reduced appetite, or digestive issues may benefit from CBD oil, which is thought to stimulate hunger in some cases.

Notes:

Guidelines for Use

Introducing CBD oil to your senior cat's care routine requires careful consideration and close monitoring.

Steps for Safe Use:

- ***Consult Your Veterinarian:*** Always discuss the use of CBD oil with your veterinarian before introducing it to your cat's regimen. They can help you determine if it's appropriate based on your cat's health history, existing medications, and specific needs.
- ***Start with a Low Dose:*** Begin with the lowest recommended dose for your cat's weight and gradually increase if needed. Monitor your cat closely for any side effects, such as lethargy, changes in appetite, or gastrointestinal upset.
- ***Choose High-Quality Products:***
    - Opt for CBD products specifically formulated for pets.
    - Ensure the product is free from THC (tetrahydrocannabinol), the psychoactive compound in cannabis, as it is toxic to cats.
    - Look for products with third-party lab testing to confirm purity, potency, and the absence of harmful contaminants.
- ***Monitor Progress:*** Keep a journal of your cat's behavior, pain levels, and overall condition while using CBD oil. Share this information with your veterinarian to assess its effectiveness and make any necessary adjustments.

Notes:

Precautions and Potential Side Effects

While CBD oil is generally considered safe, it's important to be aware of potential risks and side effects.

Possible Side Effects:

- Drowsiness or lethargy, especially if the dose is too high.
- Diarrhea or upset stomach in rare cases.
- Changes in appetite or thirst.

Precautions:

- Avoid combining CBD with other medications without veterinary guidance, as it may interact with certain drugs.
- Store CBD products in a cool, dark place to preserve their potency and effectiveness.

CBD oil can be a valuable addition to your senior cat's care plan, offering relief from pain and anxiety while promoting relaxation and overall comfort. By following guidelines for safe use and consulting with your veterinarian, you can harness the potential benefits of CBD to improve your cat's quality of life in their golden years.

Notes:

Herbal Remedies

Herbal medicine has been used for centuries to address a variety of ailments in humans and animals alike. When used properly, some herbs and natural supplements can offer safe, gentle support for your cat's health and well-being, particularly during times of stress, aging, or illness.

Common Options:

- ***Chamomile:*** Known for its calming and anti-inflammatory properties, chamomile can ease anxiety, promote relaxation, and even soothe minor digestive upset.
- ***Glucosamine and Chondroitin:*** These natural supplements are beneficial for joint health, reducing stiffness, inflammation, and pain in aging or arthritic cats, helping to improve mobility and comfort.
- ***Valerian Root:*** Acts as a natural sedative, helping to calm hyperactive or stressed cats. It can also aid in reducing aggression or restlessness in multi-cat households.
- ***Licorice Root:*** Often used as an anti-inflammatory, this herb may support cats with allergies, respiratory issues, or digestive discomfort.
- ***Slippery Elm Bark:*** A safe option for digestive health, it can soothe an irritated stomach or help manage constipation or diarrhea.
- ***Milk Thistle:*** Known for its liver-supportive properties, milk thistle may help detoxify and protect the liver in cats with chronic liver disease or after exposure to toxins.

Notes:

Herbal Remedies

Safety Tips:

- Only use veterinarian-recommended herbal remedies, as some herbs (e.g., garlic, onion, and pennyroyal) are toxic to cats and can cause serious harm.
- Avoid over-the-counter supplements meant for humans, as dosages and ingredients may not be safe or appropriate for feline use.
- Administer herbal remedies in the correct form and dosage, as cats are particularly sensitive to certain substances. Tinctures without alcohol are often safer than dried or powdered forms.
- Monitor your cat closely for any adverse reactions, such as vomiting, lethargy, or changes in appetite, and discontinue use if symptoms occur.
- Purchase high-quality, organic herbal products specifically labeled for pet use to ensure they are free from contaminants or harmful additives.

Notes:

"Holistic and alternative therapies for cats honor their natural wisdom, nurturing their well-being through gentle, balanced care."

Aromatherapy

Essential oils, when used with caution and knowledge, can create a relaxing environment for your cat. They may support emotional well-being, especially during stressful or unsettling times. However, aromatherapy must always prioritize safety due to cats' heightened sensitivity to essential oils.

Benefits:

- ***Stress Reduction:*** Scents like lavender, chamomile, and valerian root can help soothe cats during stressful situations, such as vet visits, travel, thunderstorms, or household changes.
- ***Mood Improvement:*** Creating a calm, aromatic environment can enhance your cat's overall quality of life, particularly for cats suffering from anxiety, restlessness, or agitation.
- ***Enhanced Sleep:*** Gentle scents like sandalwood and cedarwood can promote relaxation and restful sleep, particularly for senior cats or those with chronic conditions.
- ***Appetite Stimulation:*** Certain essential oils, used appropriately, may help improve a cat's appetite during illness or recovery.

Notes:

Aromatherapy

Safety Tips:

- Avoid oils that are toxic to cats, such as tea tree, citrus, eucalyptus, peppermint, and clove, as they can cause severe adverse reactions.
- Always use a high-quality diffuser in a well-ventilated area to ensure the aroma disperses gently and evenly, avoiding any concentrated exposure.
- Allow your cat the choice to leave the area if they find the scent overwhelming or unpleasant.
- Never apply essential oils directly to your cat's skin or fur, as their skin is highly sensitive, and oils can lead to irritation, toxicity, or even poisoning.
- Consult your veterinarian before using aromatherapy, particularly if your cat has existing medical conditions or is on medications.
- Limit aromatherapy sessions to short periods, such as 15–20 minutes, and observe your cat's behavior closely to ensure they are comfortable.
- Store essential oils in a secure place away from your cat's reach to prevent accidental ingestion or spills.

Notes:

Hydrotherapy

Though less common for cats, hydrotherapy can be highly beneficial for specific conditions, providing a gentle, low-impact way to address physical and health issues. This water-based therapy can promote healing, enhance mobility, and improve the overall quality of life for your feline companion.

Applications:

- Cats recovering from surgeries, such as orthopedic procedures or spinal injuries, may benefit significantly from hydrotherapy to regain strength, mobility, and muscle tone.
- Warm water immersion can help soothe sore joints, reduce inflammation, and improve circulation, making it beneficial for aging cats or those with arthritis.
- Hydrotherapy can also aid in weight management by encouraging physical activity in a low-stress environment.
- It may help cats with neurological conditions or muscle atrophy by providing a controlled setting for rebuilding coordination and strength.

Considerations:

- Use specially designed pools, treadmills, or other equipment tailored for feline hydrotherapy to ensure the therapy is both effective and safe.
- Always work with a professional experienced in hydrotherapy for cats who can assess your cat's specific needs and develop a personalized treatment plan.
- Introduce your cat to the therapy gradually, as many felines may initially be apprehensive about water-based treatments.
- Ensure the water temperature is carefully monitored and adjusted to suit your cat's comfort and health needs.
- Regularly evaluate the progress with your hydrotherapy practitioner and veterinarian to make adjustments as needed for optimal results.

Notes:

Energy Therapies

Energy-based healing methods, though not scientifically proven, can provide relaxation, comfort, and emotional support. These methods are often gentle and non-invasive, making them suitable for sensitive or ailing animals.

Reiki:

- Reiki practitioners use their hands to channel positive energy into the cat, promoting balance, healing, and a sense of calm.
- This therapy may help reduce stress, alleviate discomfort, and improve overall well-being in a dying or sick cat.
- While results vary, many pet owners report noticeable improvements in their cat's mood, energy levels, and ability to relax during their final days.
- Reiki sessions can often be tailored to the unique needs of your pet, creating a soothing environment during a difficult time.

Considerations:

- Seek out a certified practitioner who specializes in working with animals, as they understand the specific needs and sensitivities of pets.
- Always consult with your veterinarian before starting any complementary therapy to ensure it aligns with your cat's medical care plan.
- Consider observing a session beforehand to ensure you're comfortable with the practitioner's approach and techniques.
- Regular sessions may be more effective than a one-time treatment, so discuss a plan with the practitioner for ongoing support.

Notes:

Combining Therapies for Maximum Comfort

Holistic care is most effective when therapies complement one another. For instance:

- Pairing acupuncture with massage therapy can enhance pain relief.
- Using CBD alongside herbal remedies can provide comprehensive support for anxiety or inflammation.

Always consult with your veterinarian to create a coordinated treatment plan that avoids overstimulation or conflicts between therapies.

Monitoring Progress

Tracking your cat's responses to these therapies is crucial for long-term success. Maintain a journal to note:

- Changes in pain levels, behavior, and activity.
- Any side effects or adverse reactions to treatments.
- Feedback from your veterinarian on the effectiveness of each approach.

Holistic and alternative therapies offer a compassionate way to address the challenges of aging and chronic illness in cats. By focusing on their physical comfort, emotional well-being, and overall quality of life, you can ensure that your senior cat's golden years are as peaceful and fulfilling as possible. Always approach these methods with care and the guidance of a trusted veterinarian.

Notes:

"Pet cats are the guardians of our quiet moments, filling our lives with grace, mystery, and unconditional love."

04 Recognizing Signs of Decline

- Physical Indicators of Decline...76
- Behavioral Changes in End-of-Life Stages...79
- Emotional Support for Your Cat...80
- When to Consider Veterinary Intervention...80

Chapter Four
Recognizing Signs of Decline

As cats approach the final stages of their lives, recognizing the signs of decline becomes a vital responsibility for pet owners. These signs may manifest gradually or suddenly, and being attuned to them can significantly improve your cat's comfort and quality of life. Understanding these subtle and sometimes overt changes ensures that you can respond with timely, compassionate care, allowing your feline companion to experience peace and dignity in their twilight years.

The process of decline is not uniform; every cat's journey is unique. Some cats may show physical symptoms such as loss of appetite, labored breathing, or reduced mobility, while others exhibit behavioral changes, such as seeking isolation or displaying confusion. By learning to identify these signs, you can better anticipate their needs and create a supportive, loving environment.

This chapter offers a comprehensive guide to recognizing the physical, behavioral, and emotional indicators of a cat nearing the end of their life. It also provides practical advice on how to care for them during this time, including tips on creating a comfortable space, ensuring proper hydration, managing pain, and providing emotional support. The goal is to empower you to make informed decisions about their care, including when to seek veterinary intervention or consider options like palliative care or euthanasia.

By approaching this sensitive time with empathy and preparation, you can honor the bond you share with your cat. This guide will help you navigate the complexities of their end-of-life journey, ensuring that their final days are marked by love, comfort, and respect. Through your attentive care, you can give your beloved companion the dignity they deserve as they transition through this natural, yet emotional, phase of life.

Physical Indicators of Decline

Loss of Appetite

A marked decrease in appetite is often an early indication that your cat's body is beginning to slow down. This can stem from underlying illnesses or simply the natural progression of aging and nearing the end of life.

What You Can Do:

- Offer foods that are easy to eat and appealing, such as high-quality wet food, baby food (without toxic ingredients like onions), or warmed-up meals to enhance the aroma.
- If your cat refuses solid food, consult your veterinarian about liquid diets or appetite stimulants that might encourage eating.
- Monitor their hydration levels carefully; dehydration can worsen their condition. If they are unable to drink, syringe-feed water or electrolyte solutions as directed by your vet.

Lethargy

Cats approaching the end of their lives often exhibit profound fatigue, sleeping most of the day and losing interest in play or interaction.

What You Can Do:

- Create a calm, quiet space for your cat to rest, ensuring they are not disturbed by household noise or activity.
- Avoid forcing interactions; instead, let your cat dictate the pace and level of engagement.

Notes:

continued...

Labored Breathing

Shallow, irregular, or labored breathing is a common sign that the body is struggling and nearing its final stages.

What You Can Do:

- Place your cat in a well-ventilated area that is free of strong odors, dust, or smoke, as these can aggravate breathing issues.
- Consult your veterinarian about medications or supplemental oxygen therapy to ease their breathing difficulties.

Incontinence

In the final stages, cats may lose control of their bladder or bowels, leading to accidents that can cause discomfort or skin irritation.

What You Can Do:

- Use soft, washable, and absorbent bedding to keep your cat comfortable and make cleanup easier.
- Gently clean your cat using a damp cloth and pat them dry to prevent irritation or infections. Consider applying a pet-safe barrier cream if recommended by your vet.

Notes:

"Recognizing the signs of decline in cats is a heartfelt duty, guiding us to support them with tenderness and understanding."

Behavioral Changes in End-of-Life Stages

Seeking Isolation

It's instinctive for many cats to withdraw to a quiet, hidden place when they sense the end is near.

What You Can Do:

- Allow your cat the freedom to retreat, but ensure the location they choose is safe, accessible, and free from hazards like sharp objects or cold drafts.
- Provide comforting items, such as a favorite blanket, toy, or something that carries your scent, to offer reassurance.

Increased Vocalization

Some cats become more vocal, meowing, yowling, or crying as they experience discomfort or confusion.

What You Can Do:

- Stay close by and speak softly to soothe your cat. Gentle petting can help them feel reassured.
- If vocalizations seem related to pain or anxiety, consult your vet about appropriate medications to alleviate discomfort.

Disorientation

Disorientation may manifest as wandering aimlessly, bumping into furniture, or forgetting familiar routines like where their litter box or food is located.

What You Can Do:

- Minimize changes in their environment to reduce stress. Avoid moving furniture or introducing new pets.
- Use nightlights to help them navigate darker spaces.
- If they seem lost or confused, gently guide them to food, water, or the litter box.

Emotional Support for Your Cat

Stay Present
Your presence can be immensely comforting to your cat. Spending quiet time with them, speaking softly, and simply being there can provide a sense of security.

Offer Gentle Touch
If your cat tolerates it, gentle massages or light strokes along their shoulders and head can ease tension and foster connection. Be mindful of their body language and stop if they seem uncomfortable.

When to Consider Veterinary Intervention

While it's natural to want to provide care at home, certain signs warrant professional intervention:

- Persistent, unmanageable pain that home care cannot alleviate.
- Severe respiratory distress or extreme difficulty breathing.
- Seizures or severe neurological symptoms, such as uncontrollable twitching or loss of coordination.

A veterinarian can help assess your cat's condition and discuss options, including palliative care, hospice, or euthanasia, to ensure their final days are as comfortable as possible.

Preparing for the End Recognizing these signs and responding with care ensures your cat's final days are filled with peace, dignity, and love. By being attuned to their needs, you can honor their life while providing the comfort and support they deserve in their twilight hours.

Notes:

"Pet cats bring a unique blend of independence and affection, making every moment shared with them a treasure."

05
End-of-Life Care Options

- Understanding Palliative Care...86
- The Process and Considerations of Euthanasia...87
- Choosing between Palliative Care and Euthanasia...89

Chapter Five
End-of-Life Care Options

Facing the end of a beloved cat's life is one of the most emotionally challenging and heart-wrenching experiences a pet owner can go through. It is a journey that requires immense courage, compassion, and thoughtful decision-making. When a cat reaches the final stages of its life, whether due to age, illness, or unforeseen circumstances, the responsibility of ensuring their comfort and dignity lies entirely with their caretaker. This period is often filled with uncertainty, as pet owners struggle to discern the best course of action that balances their emotional attachment with the practical considerations of their cat's well-being and quality of life.

Decisions surrounding end-of-life care for a cat require careful, deliberate thought and a deep understanding of your pet's physical and emotional state. It involves evaluating various factors, such as pain management, mobility, appetite, hydration, and overall mental health, to determine what constitutes a good quality of life for your unique companion. This process is not solely about prolonging life but ensuring that the time your cat has left is meaningful, free from unnecessary suffering, and filled with love and comfort. It also requires open communication with a trusted veterinarian, who can provide insights into your cat's condition, help identify symptoms of distress and offer professional guidance on available care options.

This chapter delves into the two main approaches to end-of-life care for cats: palliative care and euthanasia. Palliative care focuses on maintaining your cat's comfort and quality of life for as long as possible through medical interventions, environmental modifications, and attentive caregiving. It is often the preferred option for pet owners who wish to spend as much time as they can with their cat, cherishing the moments that remain while alleviating pain and discomfort. On the other hand, euthanasia is a compassionate choice that involves humanely ending your cat's life to prevent further suffering when their condition becomes unbearable or unmanageable. While this decision is profoundly difficult, it is often made with the utmost love and selflessness to prioritize the cat's welfare above all else.

Understanding Palliative Care

Palliative care focuses on providing comfort and managing symptoms without attempting to cure the underlying condition. This approach allows your cat to remain at home in a familiar environment, surrounded by the people and comforts they love.

Key Components of Palliative Care:

- ***Pain Management:*** Administer medications prescribed by your veterinarian to alleviate pain and discomfort.
- ***Nutritional Support:*** Offer foods that are easy to eat and appealing to encourage nourishment, even in small amounts.
- ***Hydration:*** Ensure your cat has access to fresh water and consider subcutaneous fluids if recommended by your vet.
- ***Environmental Adjustments:*** Create a warm, quiet, and easily accessible space where your cat can rest.
- ***Emotional Comfort:*** Spend quality time with your cat, providing gentle affection and reassurance.

Advantages of Palliative Care:

- Allows your cat to stay in their home, reducing stress.
- Provides an opportunity to cherish remaining time together.
- Can be customized to your cat's specific needs and preferences.

Challenges of Palliative Care:

- Requires a significant time commitment and vigilance from the caregiver.
- Managing symptoms such as pain or incontinence may become difficult as your cat's condition worsens.
- It may be hard to determine when your cat's quality of life has declined to an unacceptable level.

Notes:

The Process and Considerations of Euthanasia

Euthanasia is a humane option to prevent suffering when a cat's condition becomes untreatable or when their quality of life deteriorates significantly. While the decision to euthanize is deeply personal, many pet owners find solace in knowing they can provide their cat with a peaceful and pain-free passing.

How Euthanasia Works:

- ***Consultation:*** Your veterinarian will discuss your cat's condition and help you decide if euthanasia is the best option.
- ***Preparation:*** You may choose to be present during the procedure, which typically begins with a sedative to relax your cat.
- ***Final Injection:*** A medication is administered that peacefully stops your cat's heart and breathing.

Benefits of Euthanasia:

- Prevents prolonged suffering and ensures a painless end.
- Provides a controlled and peaceful environment for your cat's passing.
- Can be performed at home by a mobile veterinarian, offering added comfort.

Emotional Considerations:

- Feelings of guilt and grief are normal; allow yourself time to process these emotions.
- Remember that choosing euthanasia is an act of love and compassion to prevent suffering.

Notes:

"End-of-life care options for cats are a sacred choice, ensuring their final days are filled with comfort, dignity, and love."

Choosing Between Palliative Care and Euthanasia

The decision to choose between palliative care and euthanasia is one of the most profound and difficult moments in your journey with a beloved cat. Both options are acts of compassion aimed at alleviating suffering and ensuring dignity, but the choice requires a delicate balance of emotional strength, understanding, and support.

Considerations for Palliative Care

Palliative care is ideal when your cat's condition allows them to maintain some quality of life with proper management and adjustments. This approach emphasizes making their remaining time as comfortable and enriching as possible.

- ***Assessing Quality of Life:*** Use a quality-of-life scale, such as the HHHHHMM Scale (Hurt, Hunger, Hydration, Hygiene, Happiness, Mobility, More good days than bad). This tool helps objectively evaluate your cat's well-being in different areas.
- ***Commitment:*** Palliative care requires significant time and effort, including medication administration, maintaining hygiene, and regular monitoring of your cat's condition. Ensure you can commit to the demands of caregiving.
- ***Veterinary Guidance:*** Maintain close communication with your veterinarian to adjust care plans as your cat's needs evolve.
- ***End-of-Life Planning:*** Understand that palliative care may eventually transition to euthanasia if your cat's suffering outweighs their enjoyment of life.

Deciding on Euthanasia

Euthanasia is often considered when a cat's suffering cannot be alleviated through palliative care or when their quality of life deteriorates significantly. It is a deeply personal choice, often made with the guidance of a trusted veterinarian.

- ***Recognizing Unmanageable Suffering:*** Signs such as unrelieved pain, persistent vomiting, severe weight loss, or labored breathing indicate that euthanasia may be the most compassionate choice.
- ***Timing:*** While there may never feel like a "right time," waiting too long can prolong unnecessary suffering. Consider planning ahead to allow for a calm, peaceful environment.
- ***Peaceful Passing:*** Euthanasia offers a gentle and controlled way for your cat to transition, often free of fear or discomfort.

Choosing Between Palliative Care and Euthanasia

The Emotional Process

- ***Guilt and Grief:*** It is natural to feel guilt when making such a significant decision but remember that your choice is rooted in love and compassion. Allow yourself to grieve and seek support from friends, family, or pet loss counselors.
- ***Validation:*** Acknowledge the bond you shared with your cat and the care you provided throughout their life. Your efforts have ensured they felt loved and valued every step of the way.

Seeking Support

- ***Veterinary Team:*** Lean on your veterinarian for guidance and support throughout the decision-making process.
- ***Support Groups:*** Many communities and online forums are dedicated to pet loss, offering a space to share your feelings and find understanding.
- ***Memorialization:*** Honoring your cat's memory through keepsakes, photos, or rituals can provide solace and help celebrate their life.

Notes:

Choosing Between Palliative Care and Euthanasia

By carefully weighing the available options and seeking professional advice from trusted veterinarians or pet hospice specialists, you can approach this delicate decision-making process with clarity and confidence. Understanding your cat's specific needs and limitations, along with their physical and emotional well-being, is essential to making a choice that truly prioritizes their comfort and dignity. This means paying attention to signs of pain, distress, or reduced quality of life, as well as considering the treatments or interventions that could alleviate their suffering without prolonging discomfort.

Taking the time to evaluate all aspects of their care—whether palliative or involving the option of euthanasia—ensures that your decision is both informed and deeply compassionate. In addition to consulting professionals, engaging in open conversations with family members or others involved in your cat's life can provide emotional support and additional perspectives. This collaborative approach helps ensure that your cat's final days are not only free from unnecessary suffering but also enriched with love, warmth, and the reassurance of your presence.

Ultimately, the goal is to honor your bond with your cat by creating an environment where they feel safe, cherished, and valued, even in their final moments. Whether through tender caregiving at home or by making the courageous choice to end their suffering humanely, your actions will reflect your unwavering commitment to their well-being. By prioritizing their comfort and dignity, you can transform this challenging period into a time of profound connection and farewell, ensuring their final days are filled with love, compassion, and peace.

Notes:

"Pet cats are fleeting companions, leaving quiet pawprints on our lives and hearts that linger long after they're gone."

06
Coping with the Loss of a Beloved Cat

- Grieving the Loss and Understanding Emotions...96
- Memorializing Your Cat...98
- Supporting Children through Loss...99
- Supporting Other Pets through Loss...102
- Self-Care After Loss...104

Chapter Six
Coping with the Loss of a Beloved Cat

Losing a cat is one of the most profound emotional challenges a pet owner can face. Cats are not just pets; they are companions, confidants, and family members who provide unwavering comfort and joy. The bond shared with a feline companion is unique, forged through trust, affection, and countless memories that create a lasting impact. Every soft purr, playful moment, or quiet presence by your side weaves into the fabric of your daily life, creating an irreplaceable connection. When this bond is broken by loss, it can leave an overwhelming sense of grief and emptiness, making it difficult to adjust to life without their cherished companionship.

Each cat brings an irreplaceable presence into our lives, offering unconditional love, a sense of routine, and moments of pure joy that brighten even the darkest days. Their unique personalities, from their mischievous antics to their soothing companionship, create a bond that is deeply personal and irreplaceable. When a cat passes away, it is not just the loss of a pet but also the absence of a beloved presence that brought comfort, laughter, and love to your home. Their loss can leave a significant void, one that is often felt in the smallest, quietest moments, such as an empty favorite spot or the absence of their greeting when you walk through the door.

This chapter provides a comprehensive guide to navigating grief, understanding the emotional and psychological journey of loss, and finding meaningful ways to honor and cherish your cat's memory. It offers tools to cope with the various stages of grief, from denial and guilt to eventual acceptance, while providing practical suggestions for memorializing your cat in ways that celebrate the unique and enduring impact they had on your life. Additionally, this chapter seeks to remind pet owners that grieving is a natural and necessary process, one that reflects the depth of love shared with their feline friend. By acknowledging the pain of loss while embracing the cherished memories, this chapter aims to help you find a path to healing and peace.

Grieving the Loss and Understanding Emotions

Grief is a deeply personal and natural response to loss. It manifests differently for everyone and can be influenced by the circumstances surrounding your cat's death, the depth of your bond, and your individual coping mechanisms.

Grieving the loss of a pet is just as valid as mourning a human loved one.

The Emotional Spectrum: Grief may bring waves of sadness, guilt, anger, and even relief—especially if your cat endured prolonged suffering. These feelings are normal and part of the healing process.

The Importance of Self-Compassion: Accept that grief is a journey, not a destination, and give yourself permission to feel without judgment.

Stages of Grief

The grieving process often includes several emotional stages. You may not experience them in a specific order, and some stages may overlap or repeat.

- ***Denial:*** You may find it hard to accept that your beloved cat is truly gone. This is especially common if their passing was unexpected or sudden.
- ***Anger:*** Feelings of frustration or blame may arise. You might direct your anger at yourself, others, or even the illness that claimed your cat.
- ***Bargaining:*** Thoughts of "If only I had done more..." or "What if I had noticed sooner?" are natural attempts to make sense of the loss.
- ***Depression:*** Deep feelings of sadness and emptiness may take hold as the reality of your cat's absence sinks in.
- ***Acceptance:*** Over time, you may come to terms with the loss and find peace in the memories of your time together.

Notes:

Dealing with Guilt
Pet owners often grapple with guilt, questioning decisions made during their cat's final days. This guilt can be overwhelming but is typically rooted in love and a desire to do what's best for your pet.

- ***Reframing Guilt:*** Understand that your actions came from a place of compassion and care. Trust that you made the best choices possible with the information and resources you had at the time.

- ***Seeking Perspective:*** Talking to a trusted friend, family member, or counselor who understands pet loss can help you process and release feelings of guilt.

Normalizing Your Feelings
Grief is not a linear process. Emotions may ebb and flow, and certain memories, anniversaries, or even small reminders may trigger waves of sadness. Allow yourself to feel without suppressing or rushing the process. Remember, healing looks different for everyone.

Notes:

Memorializing your cat

Honoring your cat's memory can be a healing part of the grieving process. Creating a tribute allows you to celebrate their life and the joy they brought into yours.

Ideas for Memorials

- ***Keepsakes:*** Assemble a scrapbook, photo album, or shadow box filled with cherished photos, mementos, and tokens of your time together.
- ***Artwork:*** Commission a painting, sculpture, or personalized piece that reflects your cat's spirit and personality.
- ***Memorial Items:*** Preserve their pawprint in clay, engrave their name on a piece of jewelry, or display a memorial stone in their honor.
- ***Planting:*** Dedicate a tree, flower bed, or garden space as a living tribute to your cat.
- ***Tattoos:*** Some pet owners choose to get a tattoo symbolizing their cat's impact on their lives, such as a pawprint, name, or meaningful design.

Memorial Services: Host a gathering to share stories, light candles, or perform a meaningful ritual, such as scattering their ashes in a favorite spot.

Online Memorials: Many websites offer platforms for creating digital memorials where you can share photos, memories, and messages with others who understand your loss.

Notes:

Supporting Children through Loss

For children, the loss of a pet can be their first significant experience with death, which may bring confusion, sadness, or fear. Supporting them through this process with compassion and understanding is essential to helping them process their emotions and learn about loss in a healthy way.

Be Honest: Children need straightforward and truthful explanations to make sense of what has happened. Use clear, age-appropriate language. Avoid euphemisms like "went to sleep," which can be confusing or frightening. Instead, explain gently but directly that their pet has died, emphasizing that it's natural and part of life's cycle.

Encourage Expression: Provide a safe space for children to share their feelings openly. Let them know that all emotions, whether sadness, anger, or confusion, are okay. Encourage them to ask questions and answer them honestly, even if the answers are difficult. Validating their feelings can make them feel supported and less alone in their grief.

Create Rituals: Rituals can help children honor their pet's memory and find closure. Engage them in activities that feel meaningful, such as:

- Writing a letter or drawing a picture to express their love for the pet.
- Making a scrapbook or photo album filled with cherished memories.
- Planting a tree or flower in the pet's memory to create a living tribute.
- Hosting a small memorial ceremony where they can share stories and say goodbye.

Be Patient with Questions: Children may repeatedly ask the same questions about the pet's death, as they process the loss over time. Answer with patience and consistency, even if it feels repetitive.

Notes:

Supporting Children through Loss

Read Together: Sharing age-appropriate books about pet loss and grief can provide comfort and a sense of understanding. Stories can help children realize they're not alone and give them language to express their feelings.

Model Healthy Grieving: Show children that it's okay to grieve and share your emotions. Letting them see you feel sad or reminisce fondly about the pet helps them understand that their feelings are normal and shared.

Address Fears: If the pet's death raises fears about their own mortality or the loss of others they love, provide reassurance. Help them understand the pet's death in the context of age, illness, or injury, while reinforcing that they and their family members are safe.

By approaching the loss with honesty, empathy, and shared rituals, children can process their grief in a way that fosters emotional resilience and strengthens family bonds.

Notes:

"Coping with the loss of a beloved cat means honoring their memory with gratitude, while allowing yourself the grace to grieve."

Supporting Other Pets through Loss

The loss of a companion animal can deeply affect the emotional well-being of other pets in the household. Pets form bonds with one another, and the absence of a familiar companion can lead to noticeable changes in their behavior and routine.

It's important to recognize and address these signs of grief to support them during this transition.

Lethargy or Depression: Pets may exhibit reduced energy levels, less interest in playing, or a lack of enthusiasm for social interaction. They might spend more time resting or isolating themselves, reflecting their feelings of loss.

Separation Anxiety: A pet that shared a strong bond with the deceased companion may become clingier or show signs of distress when left alone. This can include excessive whining, pacing, or destructive behaviors.

Changes in Eating Habits: Grieving pets may either lose their appetite and eat less or, conversely, overeat as a coping mechanism. Monitoring their food intake is essential to ensure they remain healthy during this difficult time.

Notes:

Supporting Other Pets through Loss

Supporting Pets Through Loss

- ***Maintain Consistent Routines:*** Pets thrive on routine, and sticking to their usual schedule for feeding, walks, playtime, and bedtime can provide a sense of stability during an otherwise confusing time.
- ***Offer Extra Affection and Attention:*** Grieving pets may seek comfort from their humans more than usual. Spend extra time with them, whether through grooming, cuddling, or gentle play, to reassure them of your presence and love.
- ***Introduce New Toys or Activities:*** Providing stimulating activities can help distract pets from their grief. Puzzle toys, interactive games, or even short training sessions can keep their minds engaged and prevent them from dwelling on their loss.
- ***Monitor for Behavioral Changes:*** Keep an eye on any new or unusual behaviors to ensure they don't develop into long-term issues. If a pet seems excessively withdrawn or shows persistent signs of distress, consult a veterinarian or animal behaviorist for guidance.
- ***Allow Them to Say Goodbye:*** If possible, let surviving pets see the body of their deceased companion. This can help them understand that their friend is gone and may reduce confusion about the absence.
- ***Encourage Social Interaction:*** If they're comfortable, providing opportunities to interact with other animals or meet new friends can help alleviate loneliness. However, introduce new pets or playmates only if and when your grieving pet seems ready.

By showing patience, love, and understanding, you can help your grieving pets navigate their loss and adjust to life without their companion. This process not only supports their healing but also strengthens your bond with them.

Notes:

Self-Care After Loss

Losing a beloved cat can be an overwhelming emotional experience, as pets are often more than companions—they are family members. Grieving can also affect your physical well-being, leading to fatigue, appetite changes, and difficulty concentrating. Taking care of yourself during this time is essential to healing and honoring your cherished bond with your pet.

Tips for Coping:

- ***Reflect:***

Take time to process your emotions and memories. Journaling can help you express feelings that may be difficult to share aloud, offering clarity and relief. Meditation or mindfulness exercises can provide moments of calm and a sense of grounding during turbulent emotions. Reflect on the joy and love your cat brought into your life, focusing on the happy moments you shared.

- **Stay Active:**

Physical activity can help alleviate stress and boost your mood. Even gentle activities, like walking or yoga, can promote mental and emotional well-being. Engaging in hobbies—whether it's painting, cooking, or gardening—can provide a healthy distraction and bring moments of joy. Spending time outdoors, surrounded by nature, can also be comforting and restorative.

- **Connect with Supportive People:**

Share your feelings with friends, family, or a support group who understand your grief. Talking about your pet, recounting memories, or simply being heard can make a significant difference. If you feel isolated, consider joining online communities or local groups for pet loss support.

- **Honor Your Pet's Memory:**

Commemorating your cat can bring comfort. Create a special tribute, such as a photo album, a memorial space in your home, or planting a tree in their honor. Sharing stories and celebrating their life can transform pain into a celebration of the love you shared.

- **Be Patient:**

Grief doesn't follow a set timeline, and everyone's journey is unique. It's important to allow yourself the time and space to heal at your own pace. Avoid self-judgment or pressure to "move on." Understand that ups and downs are part of the process, and healing takes time.

Self-Care After Loss

- **Seek Professional Support if Needed:**

If your grief feels overwhelming or persists for a prolonged period, consider reaching out to a therapist or counselor specializing in pet loss. Professional guidance can provide additional tools and support to navigate this challenging time.

By prioritizing your well-being, you not only honor your cat's memory but also nurture your own ability to heal and cherish the love they brought into your life. Grief is a testament to the bond you shared, and caring for yourself is a crucial step in honoring that connection.

Notes:

"Grieving a cat is mourning a silent soulmate, whose love lingers in every corner of your heart."

07 Moving Forward

- Moving Forward...109
- Reopening Your Heart to a New Pet...110
- Some Final Thoughts...112

Chapter Seven
Moving Forward

Grieving the loss of your cat does not mean letting go of their memory or the bond you shared. The process of healing is not about forgetting, but rather about finding ways to cherish the time you had together while opening yourself to new experiences. Over time, the intensity of pain may lessen, allowing cherished memories to resurface with warmth rather than sorrow. Each moment you spent with your cat serves as a reminder of their love, loyalty, and companionship—qualities that will remain a part of you forever. Moving forward is not an act of erasing the past; it is a process of weaving those beautiful moments into the fabric of your life as you embrace the future.

The lessons your feline companion taught you—patience, kindness, unconditional love—become a guide for how you navigate your relationships with others, both human and animal. As you reflect on your journey together, you may find comfort in small rituals, such as lighting a candle in their memory or keeping a favorite toy or photo nearby. These actions honor their place in your heart and allow you to carry their spirit with you as you move forward.

For many, the act of adopting a new pet becomes a natural and healing step. Welcoming another animal into your life can be an opportunity to channel your love and compassion toward a creature in need. However, this decision must come from a place of emotional readiness rather than societal expectations or a sense of obligation. Rushing into adopting another pet too soon may not provide the closure or peace you need. Taking the time to reflect on your feelings ensures that when you do open your heart again, it will be with genuine intention and commitment.

Reopening Your Heart to a New Pet

Timing

The journey of deciding when to welcome a new pet into your life is deeply personal. It is shaped by your emotions, your memories, and the unique relationship you shared with your beloved cat. For some, the warmth of another furry companion helps soothe the pain of loss almost immediately. For others, the process requires more time and introspection. It's essential to listen to your heart and proceed at a pace that feels right for you. There is no set timeline, and no two journeys are the same.

Honoring, Not Replacing

Welcoming a new cat doesn't diminish the special bond you had with the one you lost. Instead, it provides an opportunity to celebrate their memory by offering a safe and loving home to another animal in need. Think of it as a way to extend the love your cat taught you—your new pet will never replace the one who came before, but they will create new memories and bring their own unique joy into your life.

Adoption Considerations

When you feel emotionally ready, consider the possibility of adoption. Shelters and rescue organizations are filled with cats longing for a second chance at life. These organizations often have adult cats, seniors, or cats with special needs who might benefit most from your love and care. Adopting a pet in need not only brings companionship into your life but also honors your late cat's legacy by continuing the cycle of compassion and care.

Notes:

Some Final Thoughts

In my own journey, it took over 5 years before I felt ready to adopt another cat. During that time, I allowed myself the space to grieve, to grow, and to honor the memory of the cat I had lost. When I finally opened my heart again, I was blessed with the companionship of five wonderful cats and a lively dwarf rabbit. Each of them brings unique joy to my life, a testament to the boundless nature of love and the capacity of the heart to heal and expand. Their presence does not replace the cats I have loved and lost but instead adds new layers of meaning to the love I continue to carry with me.

It's important to trust your instincts and listen to your emotions. The right time to adopt another pet will become clear when your heart and mind are in harmony. Whether it takes weeks, months, or even years, the decision to bring another animal into your life should feel like a natural extension of the love you hold within. Trust that your journey, no matter how long, will guide you to the right moment.

Ultimately, moving forward does not mean saying goodbye to the past but rather learning to embrace the memories and lessons your beloved cat has left behind. They are a part of you, shaping the way you give and receive love. By honoring their legacy and opening your heart again when you are ready, you continue the cycle of compassion, ensuring that their spirit lives on in the connections you form with new companions.

Losing a cherished companion leaves a profound impact on your life, but it also opens a door to healing and reflection. By honoring your cat's memory, you allow yourself to cherish the bond you shared while embracing the possibility of new joy. Each moment of grief becomes a testament to the love you experienced and the happiness they brought into your life.

When you're ready, the choice to adopt another pet can become a bridge between the past and the future—a way to carry forward the lessons of compassion, care, and resilience that your feline friend left behind. While your cat's physical presence may be gone, their love and companionship will always remain a cherished part of your heart.

"Moving forward after losing a pet cat is about cherishing their memory while opening your heart to healing and the love that remains."

08 Trackers & Logs

- Daily Tracker...123
- Medication Tracker...129
- Veterinarian Visit Logs...133

COMFORT & QUALITY OF LIFE

Use the scale below to record your cat's appetite, water intake, litter box usage, and overall comfort level each day. There are no right or wrong answers. The goal is to help you identify patterns, monitor changes over time, and support discussions with your veterinarian.

10 – Excellent. Normal, healthy behavior with no noticeable concerns.

9 – Very good. Slight changes may be present but overall functioning well.

8 – Good. Mild changes observed, but daily routines remain mostly normal.

7 – Fair. Noticeable changes are present, though your cat is still managing reasonably well.

6 – Mild decline. Changes are becoming more consistent and may require closer monitoring.

5 – Moderate decline. Reduced appetite, water intake, litter box activity, or comfort is becoming more apparent.

4 – Significant decline. Daily activities are noticeably affected, and extra support may be needed.

3 – Poor. Marked changes are present, and your cat may be experiencing considerable difficulty or discomfort.

2 – Very poor. Serious concerns are present, and veterinary guidance is strongly recommended.

1 – Critical. Severe decline or distress requiring immediate veterinary attention.

DAILY TRACKER

- Appetite (10 = eating normally, 1 = refusing food)
- Water Intake (10 = drinking normally, 1 = not drinking)
- Litter Box Usage (10 = normal habits, 1 = unable or unwilling to use the litter box)
- Comfort Level (10 = relaxed and comfortable, 1 = severe discomfort)

DATE	APPETITE	WATER INTAKE	LITTER BOX USAGE	COMFORT LEVEL

DAILY TRACKER

- Appetite (10 = eating normally, 1 = refusing food)
- Water Intake (10 = drinking normally, 1 = not drinking)
- Litter Box Usage (10 = normal habits, 1 = unable or unwilling to use the litter box)
- Comfort Level (10 = relaxed and comfortable, 1 = severe discomfort)

DATE	APPETITE	WATER INTAKE	LITTER BOX USAGE	COMFORT LEVEL

DAILY TRACKER

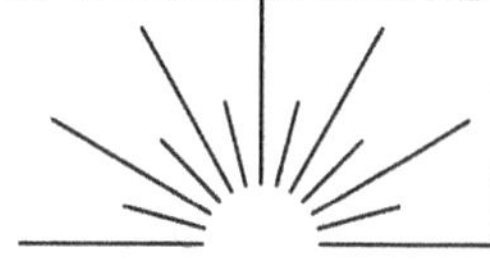

- Appetite (10 = eating normally, 1 = refusing food)
- Water Intake (10 = drinking normally, 1 = not drinking)
- Litter Box Usage (10 = normal habits, 1 = unable or unwilling to use the litter box)
- Comfort Level (10 = relaxed and comfortable, 1 = severe discomfort)

DATE	APPETITE	WATER INTAKE	LITTER BOX USAGE	COMFORT LEVEL

DAILY TRACKER

- Appetite (10 = eating normally, 1 = refusing food)
- Water Intake (10 = drinking normally, 1 = not drinking)
- Litter Box Usage (10 = normal habits, 1 = unable or unwilling to use the litter box)
- Comfort Level (10 = relaxed and comfortable, 1 = severe discomfort)

DATE	APPETITE	WATER INTAKE	LITTER BOX USAGE	COMFORT LEVEL

DAILY TRACKER

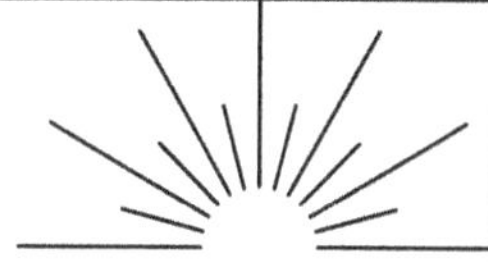

- Appetite (10 = eating normally, 1 = refusing food)
- Water Intake (10 = drinking normally, 1 = not drinking)
- Litter Box Usage (10 = normal habits, 1 = unable or unwilling to use the litter box)
- Comfort Level (10 = relaxed and comfortable, 1 = severe discomfort)

DATE	APPETITE	WATER INTAKE	LITTER BOX USAGE	COMFORT LEVEL

DAILY TRACKER

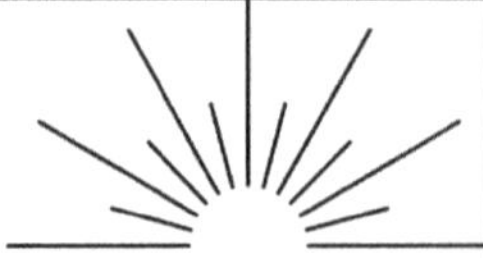

- Appetite (10 = eating normally, 1 = refusing food)
- Water Intake (10 = drinking normally, 1 = not drinking)
- Litter Box Usage (10 = normal habits, 1 = unable or unwilling to use the litter box)
- Comfort Level (10 = relaxed and comfortable, 1 = severe discomfort)

DATE	APPETITE	WATER INTAKE	LITTER BOX USAGE	COMFORT LEVEL

DAILY TRACKER

- Appetite (10 = eating normally, 1 = refusing food)
- Water Intake (10 = drinking normally, 1 = not drinking)
- Litter Box Usage (10 = normal habits, 1 = unable or unwilling to use the litter box)
- Comfort Level (10 = relaxed and comfortable, 1 = severe discomfort)

DATE	APPETITE	WATER INTAKE	LITTER BOX USAGE	COMFORT LEVEL

MEDICATION TRACKER

DATE	MEDICATION	DOSAGE	FREQUENCY	NOTES

MEDICATION TRACKER

DATE	MEDICATION	DOSAGE	FREQUENCY	NOTES

MEDICATION TRACKER

DATE	MEDICATION	DOSAGE	FREQUENCY	NOTES

MEDICATION TRACKER

DATE	MEDICATION	DOSAGE	FREQUENCY	NOTES

MEDICATION TRACKER

DATE	MEDICATION	DOSAGE	FREQUENCY	NOTES

MEDICATION TRACKER

DATE	MEDICATION	DOSAGE	FREQUENCY	NOTES

VETERINARIAN VISIT

DATE: ______________

Questions I want to ask:	
Concerns I have noticed:	
Changes since our last visit:	
Treatment options discussed:	

VETERINARIAN VISIT

DATE: ______________

Questions I want to ask:	
Concerns I have noticed:	
Changes since our last visit:	
Treatment options discussed:	

VETERINARIAN VISIT

DATE: ____________

Questions I want to ask:	
Concerns I have noticed:	
Changes since our last visit:	
Treatment options discussed:	

VETERINARIAN VISIT

DATE: ____________

Questions I want to ask:	
Concerns I have noticed:	
Changes since our last visit:	
Treatment options discussed:	

VETERINARIAN VISIT

DATE: ____________

Questions I want to ask:	
Concerns I have noticed:	
Changes since our last visit:	
Treatment options discussed:	

VETERINARIAN VISIT

DATE: ______________

Questions I want to ask:	
Concerns I have noticed:	
Changes since our last visit:	
Treatment options discussed:	

"Remembering a pet cat who has passed away is a bittersweet embrace of love, etched forever in your soul."

09 Reflection Journal

- Quality of Life Reflection...139
- Favorite Memories...146

QUALITY OF LIFE REFLECTION

As our cats grow older or face serious illness, it can be easy to focus on medications, appointments, and daily care routines. While these are important, they are only one part of the journey.

Quality of life is also measured in quieter moments: a favorite nap in a sunny window, a gentle purr, a head bump, a shared routine, or the comfort of simply being together.

The following pages are designed to help you document your cat's daily experiences and reflect on the moments that matter most. Over time, these reflections may help you recognize patterns, support conversations with your veterinarian, and create a meaningful record of your time together.

There are no right or wrong answers. Some days may bring hope and joy. Others may be difficult. The goal is not perfection, but presence.

Consider using the prompts below as a starting point:

- What brought my cat joy today?
- Did my cat seek affection or companionship?
- Did my cat seem comfortable and at ease?
- Was there a favorite activity, treat, toy, or resting place they enjoyed?
- Did I notice any changes in their mood, behavior, or routine?
- What special moment did we share today?
- What am I grateful for today?
- What do I want to remember about this day?

QUALITY OF LIFE REFLECTION

DATE: ______________

DATE: ______________

DATE: ______________

DATE: ______________

QUALITY OF LIFE REFLECTION

DATE: ____________

DATE: ____________

DATE: ____________

DATE: ____________

QUALITY OF LIFE REFLECTION

DATE: ____________

DATE: ____________

DATE: ____________

DATE: ____________

QUALITY OF LIFE REFLECTION

DATE: ____________

DATE: ____________

DATE: ____________

DATE: ____________

QUALITY OF LIFE REFLECTION

DATE: ____________

DATE: ____________

DATE: ____________

DATE: ____________

MY FAVORITE MEMORIES

very cat leaves behind a collection of memories that are uniquely their own.

Some memories make us laugh. Some bring comfort. Others become treasured stories we tell again and again. Long after the food bowls have been put away and the favorite sleeping spots sit empty, these moments remain with us.

The following pages are a place to capture the little things that made your cat special. Record favorite memories, funny stories, beloved routines, and the quirks that made them unlike any other cat in the world. Add photographs, keepsakes, or anything else that helps tell the story of your time together.

There is no right or wrong way to fill these pages. Write as much or as little as you like. The goal is simply to preserve the moments that matter most.

You may wish to reflect on:

- Funny or unforgettable memories
- Favorite photographs
- Unique personality traits and quirky habits
- Favorite toys, treats, and hiding places
- Special routines you shared together
- Ways your cat showed affection
- Lessons your cat taught you
- Things I never want to forget
- What made my cat truly one of a kind

These pages are a celebration of a life that mattered, a bond that was real, and a love that will always remain part of your story.

Favorite Memories

Favorite Memories

Favorite Memories

Favorite Memories

Favorite Memories

Online Support Groups for Pet Loss

The Rainbow Bridge Grief Support Community
A supportive online forum for those mourning the loss of their pets. Members can share their stories and provide encouragement to others.
Website: rainbowsbridge.com

The Association for Pet Loss and Bereavement (APLB)
Offers moderated chat rooms and online support sessions where you can connect with others who understand your loss.
Website: aplb.org

Reddit Pet Loss Community
A subreddit where pet owners share their grief, post memorials, and offer support to others experiencing loss.
Website: reddit.com/r/petloss

Pet Loss Support Page by ASPCA
Provides resources for dealing with grief, including a pet loss hotline and online articles.
Website: aspca.org

Grieving the Loss of a Pet Facebook Group
A private Facebook group for sharing memories and receiving comfort from other pet owners in mourning.
Website: Search on Facebook for "Grieving the Loss of a Pet."

Healing Hearts Pet Loss Support Group
An online community offering a safe space to share your grief and find compassion from others who have experienced pet loss.
Website: healingheartspetloss.com

Pet Loss Chat by Pet Compassion Careline
Provides an opportunity to connect with trained grief counselors and others experiencing similar losses.

Website: petcompassioncareline.org
Lap of Love Pet Loss Support Group
Offers virtual pet loss support groups led by trained professionals to help you navigate the grieving process.
Website: lapoflove.com

Glossary

- **Acupuncture:** A therapeutic practice involving the insertion of fine needles into specific points on the body to alleviate pain and improve overall well-being. Often used in veterinary medicine for managing chronic conditions like arthritis.
- **Aromatherapy:** The use of natural essential oils to promote relaxation or reduce anxiety. In cats, only certain oils, such as lavender and chamomile, are considered safe and should be used with caution.
- **Cannabidiol (CBD):** A compound derived from hemp that may help reduce pain, inflammation, and anxiety in cats. Always consult a veterinarian before use.
- **Cognitive Dysfunction Syndrome (CDS):** A condition in older cats characterized by behavioral changes such as confusion, altered sleep patterns, and decreased activity levels, similar to dementia in humans.
- **Euthanasia:** A humane medical procedure performed by a veterinarian to end an animal's life painlessly when suffering becomes unmanageable.
- **Feline Hospice:** A care approach that focuses on comfort and quality of life for cats nearing the end of their lives, often incorporating palliative care techniques.
- **Glucosamine and Chondroitin:** Supplements commonly used to support joint health and manage arthritis in cats.
- **Holistic Therapies:** Complementary treatments that consider a cat's overall well-being, including physical, mental, and emotional health. Examples include acupuncture, massage, and herbal remedies.
- **Hydrotherapy:** A therapeutic practice using water to relieve pain and improve mobility, typically more common in dogs but occasionally beneficial for cats.
- **Incontinence:** The inability to control urination or defecation, often seen in elderly or terminally ill cats.
- **Non-Steroidal Anti-Inflammatory Drugs (NSAIDs):** Medications prescribed by veterinarians to reduce pain and inflammation in cats. These drugs should only be used under professional guidance.
- **Palliative Care:** Medical care focused on relieving symptoms and improving the quality of life for cats with chronic or terminal conditions, rather than curing the underlying illness.
- **Quality-of-Life Scale:** A tool used by veterinarians and pet owners to assess a cat's well-being based on factors such as pain, appetite, mobility, and happiness.
- **Reiki:** An energy-healing practice that aims to promote relaxation and comfort in animals, often used as a complementary therapy.
- **Senior Cat:** A cat typically over the age of 11, with geriatric stages starting at 15 years or older. Senior cats often require specialized care and monitoring.
- **Subcutaneous Fluids:** Fluids administered under the skin to maintain hydration, commonly used in cats with chronic kidney disease or dehydration.
- **Valerian Root:** An herbal remedy that may help calm anxious cats, though it should be used sparingly and under veterinary guidance.

References

- **American Veterinary Medical Association (AVMA):** Guidelines for hospice care and euthanasia in pets. avma.org
- **International Association for Animal Hospice and Palliative Care (IAAHPC):** Resources on palliative care and quality-of-life assessment tools. iaahpc.org
- **Cornell Feline Health Center:** Comprehensive resources on senior cat health and management. vet.cornell.edu
- **The Humane Society of the United States:** Advice on coping with pet loss and honoring your pet's memory. humanesociety.org
- **Pet Loss Support Hotline:** A support resource for grieving pet owners. pet-loss.net
- **Feline Nutrition Foundation:** Diet recommendations for senior and ill cats. feline-nutrition.org
- **The Feline Veterinary Medical Association (FelineVMA):** Senior cat care guidelines and end-of-life support. catvets.com

In Memory of...

My dearest Bella, your memory is forever imprinted on my soul. I cherish the memory of your spirited nature, unwavering devotion, and boundless affection. The echo of your soft purrs and the memory of your delightful “biscuits” remain vivid, poignant reminders of the bond we share. The space where you once perched regally atop my office chair's headrest remains empty as no other can replace you.   Until we reunite in a realm beyond suffering, where your spirit soars in perfect health and joy, know that you are deeply loved and profoundly missed.

About the Author

Nafisa Zareen Khan is an author, animal lover, and lifelong advocate for treating animals with kindness, dignity, and compassion. Through her experiences caring for beloved pets, she has witnessed firsthand the profound bond that exists between humans and their animal companions, as well as the heartbreak that comes with saying goodbye.

In The Last Purr, Nafisa combines practical guidance with heartfelt understanding to help cat owners navigate one of the most difficult journeys a pet parent can face. Her goal is to provide comfort, reassurance, and support to those caring for an aging or terminally ill feline companion, while honoring the love and devotion that make these relationships so meaningful.

When she is not writing, Nafisa enjoys spending time with her family and her rescued fur babies, exploring nature, and celebrating the joy that animals bring into our lives. She believes that every cat leaves a lasting imprint on the hearts of those who love them, and that even in farewell, there is beauty, gratitude, and enduring love.

www.ingramcontent.com/pod-product-compliance
Lightning Source LLC
LaVergne TN
LVHW010609110826
845149LV00003B/832